Revolting Arithmetic: Victorians

Rowland Morgan

Revolting Arithmetic: Victorians

A smoky ironworks in Victorian times

Editor: Sarah Hall
Illustrations: Gary Clifford – The Drawing Room: pages 2, 5–7 (map), 8–10 (left), 14–16 (left and right), 26–34 (maps), 35–37 (right), 41–43 (map)
Andrew Noble – Andrew Noble Design Team Ltd: pages 3, 5–48 (top right), 5–7 (left), 8–10 (right), 11–13, 17–25, 26–28 (right), 32–37 (bottom), 38–40, 41–43 (bottom)
Layout artist: Jane Conway
Cover image: Andrew Noble
Cover design: Ed Gallagher

First published 2000 by Belair Publications, Dunstable.

Belair Publications, Albert House, Apex Business Centre, Boscombe Road, Dunstable, LU5 4RL, England.

ISBN 1–84191–038–4

Printed in Singapore by Craft Print Pte Ltd.

Contents

Phoney Talk

A Victorian telephone operator

Introduction

Cross-curricular maths

Most people agree that there is a maths problem in Britain. Pupils tend not to like it much, teachers are in short supply and results could be better. Maths is not as popular as it could be. Sadly, that has been taken for granted.

Why has maths got a bad name when, of all the subjects in primary school, maths is the one where there is often a definite right answer or a wrong one? It is the subject in which you can learn an operation, perform it and get marks. It is quite straightforward.

People use maths all the time. In a game of darts, working out a knitting pattern, checking bank accounts – there are so many ways people enjoy their command of numbers, without thinking about it.

Revolting Arithmetic takes a shot at motivating children's enjoyment of maths by integrating parts of it with history. Children will just say: cross-curricular, here we come!

How to use this book

These activities are intended to help children practise their mathematics in the context of work on historical topics. They could be used for homework or for additional mathematical work outside the daily maths lesson. You may want children to write directly on the sheets, or they may be used as resource material, with pupils recording their answers elsewhere.

To give the flexibility to match the activities to work in different year groups or to children of differing ability, the copiable activity pages are laid out in three gradations of difficulty.

Level 1 uses mathematical operations (mostly arithmetic) at a level roughly equivalent to Year 3. This should suit most children in Years 3–4. Level 2 is more appropriate to Years 4–5. Level 3 is aimed at Years 5–6.

There is a self-checking function on each sheet in which we sometimes push the agenda a little, in the hope that self-marking will motivate some stretching. You may want some children to use a calculator for this. Answers and algorithms are provided at the back of the book.

The Workshop of the World

The first twenty years of Queen Victoria's reign were the culmination of the industrial revolution that Britain pioneered. The Great Exhibition of 1851 astonished the world with its two miles of displays by 14 000 exhibitors. Nearly every factory product on earth was marked 'Made in England' (even if made in Wales, Scotland or Ireland). Britain's ironworks produced enough iron that year to build 280 Eiffel Towers. Half of it went for export. The Chartists and trades unionists on one side, and employers and financiers on the other, started forging the world's first fledgling consumer democracy. Scores of legislatures were established across the globe. Soon, the United States and Germany were competing on an industrial level; but for a generation or two, Britain was the 'workshop of the world'.

Steam Trains

Queen Victoria became queen in 1837. Steam trains were still new. The first railway line from London to Birmingham opened in eighteen hundred and thirty-eight. From Birmingham, trains went to Warrington, Liverpool and Manchester.

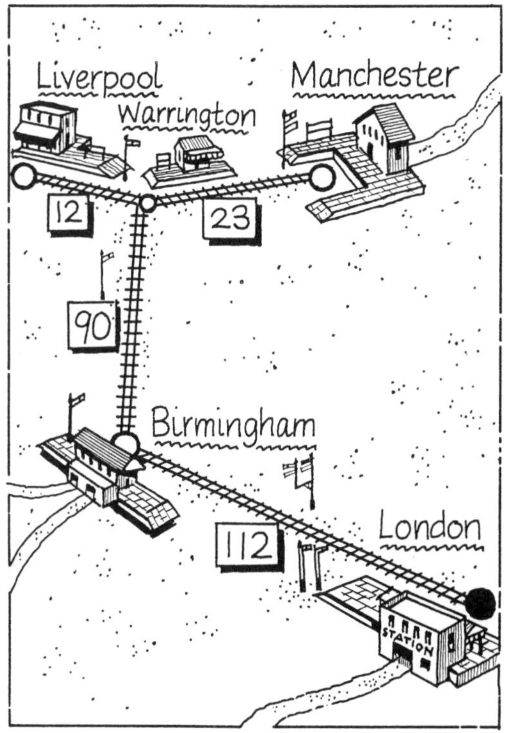

1 In what year was the London–Birmingham railway opened? Write it down in figures.

2 Look at the map. How many miles was the rail trip from Liverpool to Manchester?

3 How many miles was the rail trip from London to Warrington?

4 How many miles was a return trip London–Birmingham–London?

5 Which was further: London to Birmingham or Birmingham to Liverpool? By how many miles?

CHECK IT YOURSELF ✓

Your answer to 1 → ☐ ☐ ☐ ☐

Your answer to 2 → ☐ ☐

Your answer to 3 → **2** ☐ ☐

Your answer to 4 → **2** ☐ ☐

Your answer to 5 → ☐ ☐

Add them Result → **2** **3** ☐ ☐

Do you get **2309**? *If not, check your answers and try again.*

Steam Trains

Queen Victoria became queen in 1837. Steam trains were still new. The first railway line from London to Birmingham opened in 1838, the same year as Victoria's coronation. Using a new connection to Warrington, Londoners could reach Liverpool or Manchester. At least one service per day had to offer a ticket at one penny per mile.

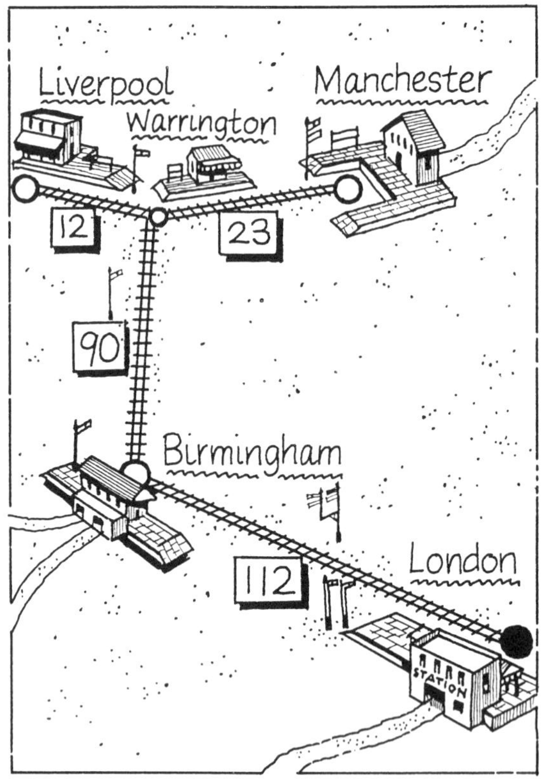

1 Look at the map. How many miles was the train ride from London to Liverpool?

2 How many miles were two return trips from Liverpool to Manchester?

3 How many miles was a return trip from London to Warrington?

4 How many miles were two return trips from London to Birmingham?

5 Which was further: from London to Birmingham return or from Birmingham to Liverpool return? By how many miles?

VICTORIAN FACT FILE

The government ordered that all trains were to have indoor seats. They were to travel at more than 15 miles per hour (24 kilometres per hour).

CHECK IT YOURSELF ✓

Your answer to 1 → ☐☐☐

Your answer to 2 → ☐☐☐

Your answer to 3 → ☐☐☐

Your answer to 4 → ☐☐☐

Your answer to 5 → ☐☐

Add them Result → ☐☐☐☐

Do you get **1226**? *If not, check your answers and try again.*

Steam Trains

Queen Victoria became queen in 1837. In Victorian times, people could travel by steam train on the newly built railways. The first railway trunk line from London to Birmingham opened in 1838, the same year as Queen Victoria's coronation. It linked London with Birmingham, 112 miles (180 kilometres) away. Using a new connection to Warrington, Londoners could reach Liverpool or Manchester, over 100 miles beyond Birmingham. At least one service per day had to offer a ticket at one penny per mile.

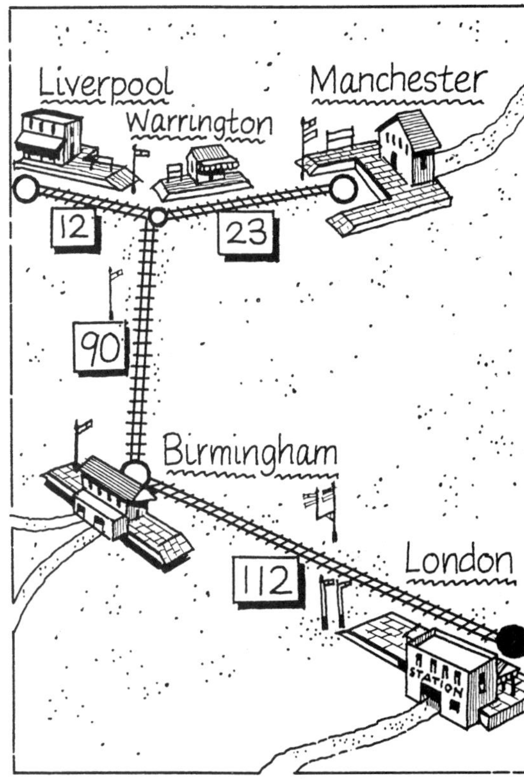

1 Look at the map. How many miles was the train ride from London to Liverpool return?

2 How many miles was the rail trip from Liverpool to Manchester return, taken every day for a week?

3 How many pence was the cheapest return ticket from London to Warrington?

4 How many miles were three return trips from London to Birmingham?

5 How many pence was the cheapest ticket from Birmingham to Liverpool return?

VICTORIAN FACT FILE
The government ordered that all trains were to have indoor seats. They were to travel at more than 15 miles per hour (24 kilometres per hour).

CHECK IT YOURSELF

Your answer to 1 → ☐☐☐

Your answer to 2 → ☐☐☐

Your answer to 3 → ☐☐☐

Your answer to 4 → ☐☐☐

Your answer to 5 → ☐☐☐

Add them Result → ☐☐☐☐

Do you get ***2198****?*
If not, check your answers and try again.

Any New Iron?

Britain, the 'workshop of the world', made two million tonnes of iron in 1850. That would have been enough to build two hundred and eighty Eiffel Towers. Half the iron went overseas. Most of the rest was used to make machines, for example railway locomotives such as the *Lord of the Isles*, which weighed 31 tonnes.

VICTORIAN FACT FILE
One Victorian ironworks was the Dowlais works in South Wales. Many rails for new railways all over the world were made there.

1 How many Eiffel Towers could the iron made in one year in Britain have built? Write the number in figures.

2 How much of Britain's iron was exported? Write the fraction in figures.

3 How many tonnes would three locomotives the size of the *Lord of the Isles* weigh?

4 How many millions of tonnes of iron per year were sent overseas? (Just write the number of millions, not all the zeros.)

CHECK IT YOURSELF

Your answer to 1 → ☐ ☐ ☐

Your answer to 3 → ☐ ☐

Your answer to 4 → ☐

Add them Result → **3** ☐ ☐

Do you get **374**?
If not, check your answers and try again.

Any New Iron?

Britain, the 'workshop of the world', made two million tonnes of iron in 1850. That would have been enough to build 280 Eiffel Towers. Half the iron was exported to the rest of the world. Much of the rest was used to make machines. One very visible machine was a huge railway locomotive, the *Lord of the Isles*, which weighed about 30 tonnes.

1 How many Eiffel Towers could two years' output of iron in Britain have built?

2 How many tonnes would a small locomotive one-third the weight of the *Lord of the Isles* weigh?

3 How many tonnes would eight locomotives the size of the *Lord of the Isles* weigh?

4 How many millions of tonnes of iron would have been made by the end of 1856? (Just write the number of millions, not all the zeros.)

VICTORIAN FACT FILE
One Victorian ironworks was the Dowlais works in South Wales which in the 1840s was one of the biggest ironworks in the world. Many rails for new railways all over the world were made there.

CHECK IT YOURSELF

Your answer to 1 → ☐☐☐

Your answer to 2 → ☐☐

Your answer to 3 → ☐☐☐

Your answer to 4 → ☐☐

Add them Result → ☐☐☐

Do you get **824**? *If not, check your answers and try again.*

Any New Iron?

Britain, the 'workshop of the world', made two million tonnes of iron in 1850. That would have been enough to build 280 Eiffel Towers. Half the iron was exported to the rest of the world, which was copying Britain's railways and machinery. Much of the other half was used to make machines for Britain's industries. Most machines were hidden from the public in factories, for example machine lathes and looms for making textiles. A typical new machine was a paper-folder that could make 2700 envelopes an hour. One very visible machine was the huge railway locomotive, the *Lord of the Isles*, which weighed about 30 tonnes.

1 How many Eiffel Towers could five years' output of iron in Britain have built?

2 How many tonnes would a locomotive three-quarters the weight of the *Lord of the Isles* weigh?

3 How much would 18 locomotives the size of the *Lord of the Isles* weigh?

4 How many envelopes would the new paper-folder have made in three hours?

VICTORIAN FACT FILE
One of the ironworks in Victorian times was the Dowlais works in South Wales which in the 1840s was one of the biggest ironworks in the world. Many rails for new railways all over the world were made there.

CHECK IT YOURSELF

Your answer to 1 → ☐☐☐☐

Your answer to 2 → ☐☐ $\frac{1}{2}$

Your answer to 3 → ☐☐☐

Your answer to 4 → ☐☐☐☐

Add them Result → ☐☐☐☐☐ $\frac{1}{2}$

Do you get **10 062 $\frac{1}{2}$**? *If not, check your answers and try again.*

Clip-clop Buses

The London Omnibus Company was started in 1858. The omnibuses were pulled by horses.

STATELLITE
The new bus company had 600 buses. A bus could take 24 passengers. It needed three horses to pull it. The company had six thousand horses.

1 How many horses did the new bus company have? Write the number in figures.

2 How many passengers could two full buses carry?

3 How many horses were needed to pull eight buses?

4 If a full bus stopped and five passengers got off, how many would be left?

5 There were two full buses. Twelve people got off one and nine off the other. How many passengers would be left on the buses?

VICTORIAN FACT FILE
The word omnibus means 'for all'. Our word *bus* comes from it.

CHECK IT YOURSELF ✓

Your answer to 1 → ☐ ☐ ☐ ☐

Your answer to 2 → ☐ ☐

Your answer to 3 → ☐ ☐

Your answer to 4 → ☐ ☐

Your answer to 5 → ☐ ☐

Add them Result → **6** **1** ☐ ☐

Do you get **6118**? *If not, check your answers and try again.*

Clip-clop Buses

The London Omnibus Company was started in eighteen hundred and fifty-eight. The omnibuses were pulled by horses.

STATELLITE
The new bus company had 600 buses. They had open-air seating on top, reached by a staircase on the outside. A bus could take 24 passengers, half upstairs, half down. Each bus was pulled by three horses, and the company had 6000 of them. The buses chiefly served the London railway stations, taking 27 000 rail travellers to work in the City on weekdays.

VICTORIAN FACT FILE
The word omnibus means 'for all'. Our word *bus* comes from it.

1 In which year was the new bus company founded? Write the number in figures.

2 How many passengers could sit upstairs?

3 How many horses were needed to pull 28 buses?

4 If a full bus came to its first stop and one-quarter of the passengers got off, how many would be left?

5 If three full buses stopped and 12 people got off each, how many passengers would be left on the buses?

CHECK IT YOURSELF

Your answer to 1 → ☐ ☐ ☐ ☐

Your answer to 2 → ☐ ☐

Your answer to 3 → ☐ ☐

Your answer to 4 → ☐ ☐

Your answer to 5 → ☐ ☐

Add them Result → **2** ☐ ☐ ☐

Do you get **2008***?*
If not, check your answers and try again.

Clip-clop Buses

The London Omnibus Company was founded in 1858. The omnibuses were pulled by horses.

STATELLITE
The new bus company had 600 buses. They looked like stagecoaches, with open-air seating on top, reached by a staircase on the outside. A bus could take 24 passengers, half upstairs, half down. Each bus was pulled by three horses, and the company had 6000 of them. They chiefly served the London railway stations, taking 27 000 rail travellers to work in the City on weekdays, but the buses were too expensive for the average manual worker.

VICTORIAN FACT FILE
The word omnibus means 'for all'. Our word *bus* comes from it.

1 How many horses were needed to pull the bus fleet?

2 If one-third of the buses served the City, how many would be left for the suburbs?

3 How many passengers could 28 buses carry?

4 If another city had an identical bus company, how many horses would the two companies own altogether?

5 If 11 full buses stopped and 12 people got off each, how many passengers would be left on the buses?

CHECK IT YOURSELF

Your answer to 1 → ☐☐☐☐

Your answer to 2 → ☐☐☐

Your answer to 3 → ☐☐☐

Your answer to 4 → ☐☐☐☐☐

Your answer to 5 → ☐☐☐

Add them   Result → ☐☐☐☐☐

Do you get **15 004**? *If not, check your answers and try again.*

Mine Martyrs

Coal was needed to make iron and steam power. It had to be carried from the coal face to the surface of the mine. Women and children brought up the coal. In 1842, the government banned the employment of women and girls, and of boys under 10 years of age in the mines.

1 After 1842, how many years too young to work was a four-year-old boy?

2 If three-quarters of the miners were men, what fraction were women and children?

3 If seven out of 23 miners were children, how many were adults?

4 If there were 180 miners in a mine and 75 of them were women, how many men were there?

5 If there were 245 children and 47 of them were under 10, how many were old enough to work in a mine?

CHECK IT YOURSELF ✓

Your answer to 1 →			☐
Your answer to 3 →		☐	☐
Your answer to 4 →	1	☐	☐
Your answer to 5 →	1	☐	☐
Add them Result →	3	☐	☐

Do you get **325**? *If not, check your answers and try again.*

Mine Martyrs

Coal was needed to make iron and steam power. It had to be carried from the coal face to the surface of the mine. Women and children brought the coal up. Children as young as four worked below ground. In 1842, the government banned the employment of females and of boys under 10 years of age in the mines.

1 If three-tenths of the miners were children, what decimal fraction of the total were adults?

2 If three-quarters of the miners were men, what decimal fraction of the total were women and children?

3 If the new law left 342 women and children out of work in one village and 247 in another, how many were without work altogether?

4 If 35 women and children lost their jobs at each of eight mines, how many new workers would have to be hired to replace them?

5 If one-third of 18 mines had children of four working, how many did not?

CHECK IT YOURSELF ✓

Your answer to 1 → **0** . ☐

Your answer to 2 → **0** . ☐ ☐

Add them/Result → **0** . ☐ ☐

Do you get **0.95**? *If not, check your answers and try again.*

Your answer to 3 → ☐ ☐ ☐

Your answer to 4 → ☐ ☐ ☐

Your answer to 5 → ☐ ☐

Add them/Result → ☐ ☐ ☐

Do you get **881**? *If not, check your answers and try again.*

Mine Martyrs

Huge amounts of coal were needed to make iron and to produce steam power. The coal was mined underground from where it had to be carried to the surface of the mine. Sometimes rail wagons pulled by ponies were used. The ponies often went blind from living in the dark. When the tunnels were too low for the ponies, women and children carried the coal to the surface. Children aged six and seven were commonly employed, and some as young as four worked below ground. In 1842, the government banned the employment of females and of boys under 10 years of age in the mines.

1 If a mine had 300 workers and half were women and children under 10, how many did the new law throw out of work?

2 If 75 out of 100 miners were men, what percentage were women and children?

3 If the new law put 2342 women and children out of work in one county and 4577 in another, how many were left without work?

4 If 35 women and children were fired at each of 18 mines, how many workers would have to be hired to replace them?

5 Out of 129 mines, if one in every three had young children working, how many did not?

VICTORIAN FACT FILE
Children also worked as door openers, opening and closing doors as the coal was taken through the tunnels. The doors helped keep the tunnels ventilated. Sometimes the children fell asleep and rolled onto the tram lines.

CHECK IT YOURSELF ✓

Your answer to 1 → ☐☐☐

Your answer to 2 → ☐☐

Your answer to 3 → ☐☐☐☐

Your answer to 4 → ☐☐☐

Your answer to 5 → ☐☐

Add them Result → ☐☐☐☐

Do you get **7810***?*
If not, check your answers and try again.

Super-ship

The steamship *Great Britain* was the first ocean liner in the world. She had a propeller and sails.

STATELLITE
SS *Great Britain* had beds for two hundred and fifty-two passengers. She first sailed in 1845, seven years after the coronation of Queen Victoria. Her first voyage was to New York. It took 14 days and 21 hours. After seven years, she started taking passengers to Australia. She stopped sailing in 1866.

1 Write down in figures how many passenger beds the ship had.

2 In what year was the coronation of Queen Victoria?

3 In what year did the ship start taking passengers to Australia?

4 For how many more years did she sail after starting a service to Australia?

5 Round to the nearest day how long it took her to reach New York.

CHECK IT YOURSELF ✓

Your answer to 1 →	☐	☐	☐
Fill in the last two figures from answer 2 →		☐	☐
Fill in the last two figures from answer 3 →		☐	☐
Your answer to 4 →		☐	☐
Your answer to 5 →		☐	☐
Add them Result →	3	☐	☐

Do you get **371**?
If not, check your answers and try again.

Super-ship

The steamship *Great Britain* was the first ocean liner in the world. She was driven by a propeller and had six masts.

STATELLITE
She was built in Bristol in eighteen hundred and forty-three. She had an iron hull 100 metres long and cost £112 000. She had beds for 252 passengers and carried another 92 without beds, as well as a cargo of 1200 tonnes. In 1845 she made her first voyage, to New York. She arrived in 14 days, 21 hours. After seven years, she began to serve on the Australia route. She was taken out of service in 1866.

1 Write in figures the year in which the SS *Great Britain* was built.

2 How many passengers could she take altogether?

3 How many hours short of 15 days was her first voyage to New York?

4 For how many years did she sail?

5 If she travelled full from London to New York and returned with another load of passengers, how many passengers did she carry altogether?

CHECK IT YOURSELF ✓

Your answer to 1 →	☐	☐	☐	☐
Your answer to 2 →		☐	☐	☐
Your answer to 3 →				☐
Your answer to 4 →			☐	☐
Your answer to 5 →		☐	☐	☐
Add them Result →	2	☐	☐	☐

Do you get ***2899****?*
If not, check your answers and try again.

Super-ship

The SS *Great Britain* was the first transatlantic liner. Steam-powered, she was driven by a propeller and had six masts.

STATELLITE
She was built in Bristol in eighteen hundred and forty-three. She had an iron hull 100 metres long. She cost £112 000, plus half as much again for the special dry dock required. She had beds for 252 passengers and carried another 92 without beds, as well as a cargo of 1200 tonnes. In 1845 she made her first voyage, to New York, arriving in 14 days, 21 hours. After seven years, she served on the Australia route. She was taken out of service in 1866.

1 If the SS *Great Britain* weighed 1110 tonnes, how much did she weigh with her cargo?

VICTORIAN FACT FILE
The SS *Great Britain* was designed by a famous engineer called Isambard Kingdom Brunel. The ship is now a tourist attraction in Bristol.

2 If she made eight trips between Bristol and New York with full passenger loads, how many passengers would she carry?

3 How much did her dry dock cost?

4 How many hours did her first cruise to New York last?

5 If a return trip to Australia took three months, how many trips could she make in seven years?

CHECK IT YOURSELF

Your answer to 1 → □□□□

Your answer to 2 → □□□□

Your answer to 3 → □□□□□

Your answer to 4 → □□□

Your answer to 5 → □□

Add them   Result → 6□□□□

Do you get **61 447**? *If not, check your answers and try again.*

Pedalling Along

The pedal bicycle appeared in Victorian times. Many people claimed to have invented it.

STATELLITE
A Frenchman named Michaux made a wooden bike in 1818. By 1865, his workshop was building four hundred per year. At first, tyres were hard. John Dunlop began selling pump-up tyres in 1888. The best bicycles cost £100 (about the same as £5000 now).

1 How many wheels are required to make 12 bicycles?

2 How many bicycles did the Michaux workshop make in six months?

3 How many pounds did three top-quality bicycles cost?

4 How many pedals are needed for nine bicycles?

VICTORIAN FACT FILE
A Victorian bicycle had its pedals fixed to the front wheel, which was bigger than the back wheel.

CHECK IT YOURSELF ✓

Your answer to 1 →		☐	☐
Your answer to 2 →	**2**	☐	☐
Your answer to 3 →	**3**	☐	☐
Your answer to 4 →		☐	☐
Add them Result →	**5**	☐	☐

Do you get **542**? *If not, check your answers and try again.*

Pedalling Along

The pedal bicycle appeared in Victorian times. Many people claimed to have invented it.

STATELLITE
A Frenchman named Michaux claimed to have produced the first bike (made of wood) in 1818. By 1865, the Michaux workshop was producing four hundred per year. At first, tyres were hard. Then in 1888, John Dunlop began selling pump-up tyres. Cycling became very popular. The best bicycles cost £100 (the equivalent of about £5000 now). They were still less expensive than a horse and carriage.

1 How many wheels are required to make 24 bicycles?

2 How many bicycles could the Michaux workshop make in three years?

3 If two friends wanted to share the cost of a top-quality bicycle, how much would they each pay?

4 How many pedals are needed for 39 bicycles?

VICTORIAN FACT FILE
A Victorian bicycle had its pedals fixed to the front wheel, which was bigger than the back wheel. The rider sat across the front wheel to pedal.

CHECK IT YOURSELF ✓

Your answer to 1 → ☐ ☐

Your answer to 2 → 1 ☐ ☐ ☐

Your answer to 3 → ☐ ☐

Your answer to 4 → ☐ ☐

Add them Result → 1 ☐ ☐ ☐

Do you get **1376***? If not, check your answers and try again.*

Pedalling Along

The pedal bicycle appeared in Victorian times.
Many people claimed to have invented it.

STATELLITE
A German baron claimed to have invented the first bike (without pedals). Then a Frenchman named Michaux claimed to have produced the first bike (made of wood) in 1818. By 1865, the Michaux workshop was producing four hundred per year. At first, tyres were hard. The pneumatic (pump-up) tyre was patented in 1846 and John Dunlop began to manufacture them in 1888. The smoother ride made cycling popular with those who could afford it. The best bicycles cost £100 (the equivalent of about £5000 now). They were still less expensive than a horse and carriage, and more convenient than either horse-drawn buses or trams.

1 How many years passed between Michaux inventing his bike and making 400 a year?

2 How many bicycles could the Michaux workshop make in nine years?

3 How many wheels are required for 392 bicycles?

4 How many years passed between the patenting of pneumatic tyres and their manufacture by John Dunlop?

5 The best bicycles cost £100. An ordinary bicycle cost about 30 per cent of the price. How much is that?

VICTORIAN FACT FILE
A Victorian bicycle had its pedals fixed to the front wheel, which was bigger than the back wheel. The rider sat astride the front wheel to pedal.

CHECK IT YOURSELF ✓

Your answer to 1 → ☐☐

Your answer to 2 → ☐☐☐☐

Your answer to 3 → ☐☐☐

Your answer to 4 → ☐☐

Your answer to 5 → ☐☐

Add them Result → ☐☐☐☐

Do you get **4503***?*
If not, check your answers and try again.

Crystal Palace

Prince Albert, the husband of Queen Victoria, wanted to display the products of the 'workshop of the world'. He planned a huge exhibition.

STATELLITE
Prince Albert turned down two hundred and forty-four building plans. Then Joseph Paxton designed an enormous greenhouse. It was three times the size of St Paul's Cathedral, covering 14 hectares. Everyone called it the Crystal Palace. The exhibition opened in London's Hyde Park in 1851.

1 How many plans did Prince Albert turn down? Write the number in figures.

2 Suppose Prince Albert ran out of money. How many hectares would the building have covered if it had been half the size?

3 Suppose the exhibition had been delayed by five years. In what year would it have opened?

4 If the building had been twice as big, how many St Paul's Cathedrals would it have held?

CHECK IT YOURSELF ✓

Your answer to 1 →		☐	☐	☐
Your answer to 2 →				☐
Your answer to 3 →	1	8	☐	☐
Your answer to 4 →				☐
Add them Result →	2	1	☐	☐

Do you get **2113**?
If not, check your answers and try again.

Crystal Palace

Prince Albert, the husband of Queen Victoria, wanted to display the products of the 'workshop of the world'. He planned a huge exhibition.

STATELLITE
Prince Albert rejected 244 building plans. Then Joseph Paxton designed an enormous greenhouse. It was three times the size of St Paul's Cathedral, covering 14 hectares, with room for two miles of exhibits. Everyone called it the Crystal Palace. The exhibition opened in London's Hyde Park in 1851. There were fourteen thousand separate exhibitors.

1 Suppose it took Prince Albert half an hour to study each rejected plan. For how many hours altogether would he have studied the proposals?

2 Suppose Prince Albert had built another three Crystal Palaces in other cities. How many hectares would all the buildings have covered?

3 Write in figures the number of exhibitors.

4 If the entry ticket cost three shillings, how many shillings did it cost for 36 people?

VICTORIAN FACT FILE
After the Great Exhibition, the Crystal Palace was moved to South London. In 1936, it caught fire and burned down. The part of London it was moved to is still called Crystal Palace.

CHECK IT YOURSELF ✓

Your answer to 1 → ☐☐☐

Your answer to 2 → ☐☐

Your answer to 3 → ☐☐☐☐☐

Your answer to 4 → ☐☐☐

Add them/Result → 1 4 ☐☐☐

Do you get **14 286**? *If not, check your answers and try again.*

Crystal Palace

Prince Albert, the husband of Queen Victoria, wanted to display the products of the 'workshop of the world'. He planned a huge exhibition.

STATELLITE
Prince Albert rejected 244 proposed buildings. Then Joseph Paxton, a landscape gardener, designed an enormous greenhouse. It was three times the size of St Paul's Cathedral, covering 14 hectares, with room for two miles of exhibits. Everyone called it the Crystal Palace. The exhibition opened in London's Hyde Park in 1851. There were 14 000 exhibitors showing their wares. It was the first major trade show ever and attracted visitors from all parts of the world.

1 Suppose Prince Albert had studied five of the building plans for an hour and a half each. How many hours would that be altogether?

2 If Prince Albert marked one-tenth of all the proposed buildings as 'possibles', how many possibles was that (to the nearest one)?

3 Suppose Prince Albert had built a further three Crystal Palaces in other cities. How many exhibitors would all the buildings have held?

4 Suppose the building had been delayed by 36 months. In what year would it have opened?

VICTORIAN FACT FILE
After the Great Exhibition, the Crystal Palace was moved from Hyde Park to South London. In 1936, it caught fire and burned down. The part of London it was moved to is still called Crystal Palace.

CHECK IT YOURSELF

Your answer to 1 → ☐ . ☐

Your answer to 2 → ☐ ☐ . 0

Your answer to 3 → ☐ ☐ ☐ ☐ ☐ . 0

Your answer to 4 → ☐ ☐ ☐ ☐ . 0

Add them Result → ☐ ☐ ☐ ☐ ☐ . ☐

Do you get **57 885.5***? If not, check your answers and try again.*

A Bright Idea

Electricity had been discovered before the Victorian Age. The first public electric lights were put up in Godalming, Surrey, in 1881. Imagine the map is part of Godalming soon after 1881.

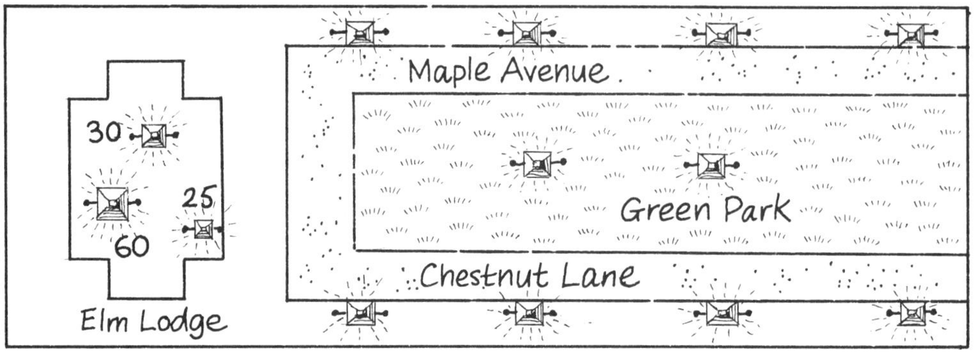

1 If Elm Lodge had one 30-watt lamp, one 25-watt lamp and one 60-watt lamp, how many watts is that altogether?

2 If they switched off the 25-watt lamp, how many watts would that leave?

3 If the lamps on Maple Avenue were each 75 watts, how many watts would that be in the whole street?

4 If each lamp on Chestnut Lane was 30 watts, how many watts would that be in the street?

5 If each lamp in Green Park was 65 watts, how many watts would that be in the park?

CHECK IT YOURSELF

Your answer to 1 →	**1**		
Your answer to 2 →			
Your answer to 3 →	**3**		
Your answer to 4 →	**1**		
Your answer to 5 →	**1**		
Add them Result →	**7**		

Do you get **755**?
If not, check your answers and try again.

A Bright Idea

Electricity had been discovered before the Victorian Age. However, it was not until 1879 that Joseph Swan demonstrated Britain's first electric light bulb. The first public lighting system was installed in 1881 in Godalming, Surrey. Imagine the map is part of Godalming soon after 1881.

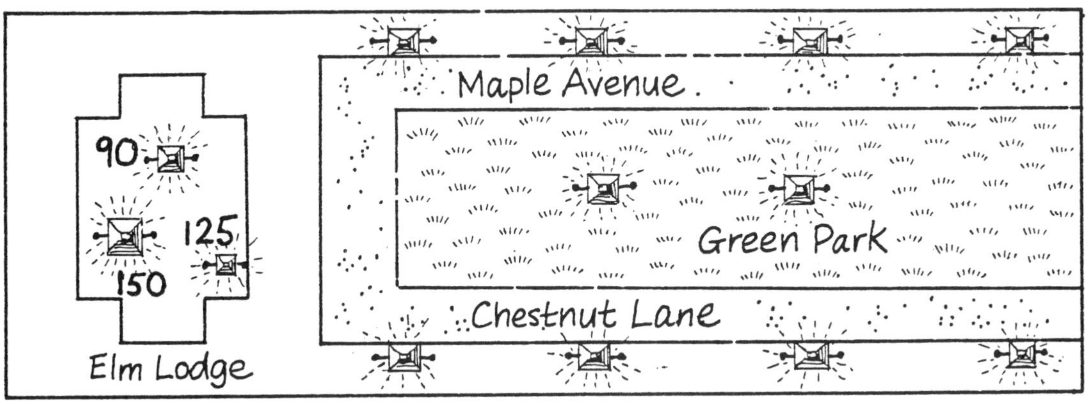

1 If Elm Lodge had one 90-watt lamp, one 125-watt lamp and one 150-watt lamp, how many watts would the lighting consume?

2 If the occupants switched off the 125-watt lamp, how many watts would be used then?

3 If the lamps on Maple Avenue and Chestnut Lane were each 75 watts, how many watts would the streets consume?

4 If another house was lit in the same way as Elm Lodge, how many watts would the two houses consume?

5 If each lamp in Green Park was 150 watts, how many watts would the lighting consume?

CHECK IT YOURSELF ✓

Your answer to 1 → ☐☐☐

Your answer to 2 → ☐☐☐

Your answer to 3 → ☐☐☐

Your answer to 4 → ☐☐☐

Your answer to 5 → ☐☐☐

Add them Result → ☐☐☐☐

Do you get **2235**?
If not, check your answers and try again.

A Bright Idea

Electricity had been discovered before the Victorian Age. However, it was not until 1879 that a member of the Newcastle Chemical Society, Joseph Swan, demonstrated Britain's first electric light bulb. The first public lighting system was installed in 1881 in Godalming, Surrey. Imagine the map is part of Godalming soon after 1881.

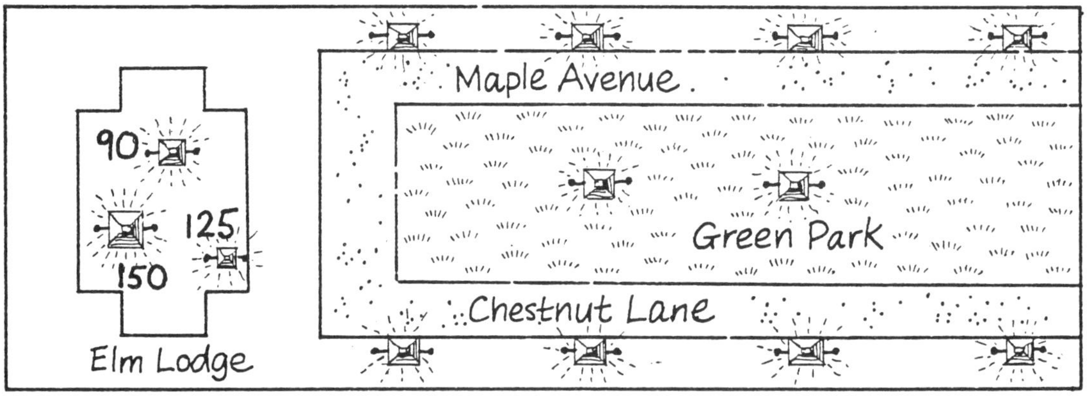

1 If there were another three large houses with the same lighting as Elm Lodge, how many watts of lighting would the houses have altogether?

2 If the occupants of Elm Lodge then switched off their 125-watt lamp, how many watts would the four houses use?

3 If six other streets had lighting like Maple Avenue and Chestnut Lane, and each lamp was 75 watts, how many watts would the streets consume altogether?

4 If the street lamps were all changed to 60 watts, how many watts would the eight streets then consume?

5 Each lamp in Green Park is 30 watts. Godalming plans another 55 pairs of park lamps like these. How many watts would all the park lamps consume?

VICTORIAN FACT FILE
Within two years of the new lights going up in Godalming, the General Post Office in Glasgow, the Mansion House in London and several big railway stations had similar systems.

CHECK IT YOURSELF ✓

Your answer to 1 → ☐☐☐☐

Your answer to 2 → ☐☐☐☐

Your answer to 3 → ☐☐☐☐

Your answer to 4 → ☐☐☐☐

Your answer to 5 → ☐☐☐☐

Add them Result → ☐☐☐☐☐

Do you get **10 475**? *If not, check your answers and try again.*

Naval Empire

Britain, the 'workshop of the world', had a huge navy. Most of its ships were based far away overseas. Look at this map. It shows the number of Royal Navy warships and where they were based in the middle of the nineteenth century.

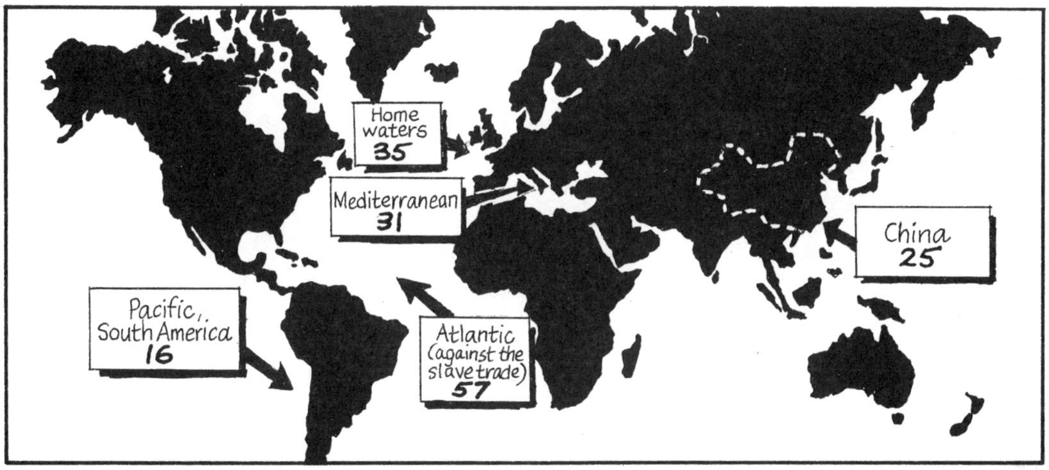

1 How many warships did the Royal Navy have overseas, not in home waters?

2 How many warships did the Royal Navy have altogether?

3 How many warships were not busy wiping out the slave trade in the Atlantic?

4 How many warships did the Royal Navy have in the Pacific Ocean (China and South America)?

CHECK IT YOURSELF ✓

Your answer to 1 →	1		
Your answer to 2 →	1		
Your answer to 3 →	1		
Your answer to 4 →			
Add them Result →	4		

Do you get **441**? *If not, check your answers and try again.*

Naval Empire

Britain, the 'workshop of the world', had a huge navy. Its ships were stationed all over the world with only 35 in home waters. Most were based far away overseas. Look at this map. It shows the number of Royal Navy warships and where they were based in the middle of the nineteenth century.

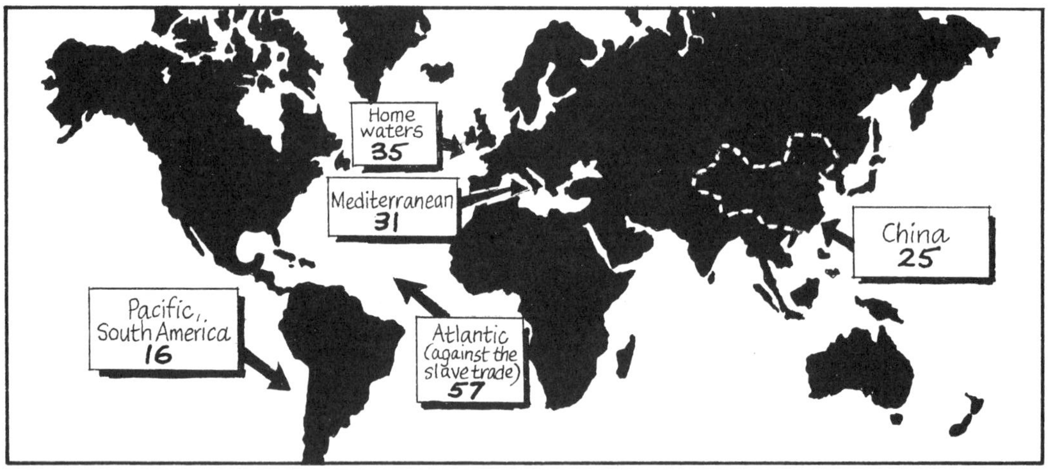

1 If each warship had two doctors, how many doctors would the Royal Navy have had on warships in the China Sea?

2 If each warship flew three flags, how many flags would the Royal Navy have flown on warships in the Atlantic?

3 How many warships did the Royal Navy have altogether?

4 If there was an emergency and the Royal Navy had to treble the number of warships in the Pacific Ocean (China and South America), how many would it have had?

CHECK IT YOURSELF ✓

Your answer to 1 → ☐☐

Your answer to 2 → ☐☐☐

Your answer to 3 → ☐☐☐

Your answer to 4 → ☐☐☐

Add them Result → ☐☐☐

Do you get **508**? *If not, check your answers and try again.*

Naval Empire

Britain, the 'workshop of the world', served its customers (and controlled its suppliers) with a huge navy. Its ships were stationed all over the world, with only 35 in home waters. Most were based far away overseas. Look at this map. It shows the number of Royal Navy warships and where they were based in the middle of the nineteenth century.

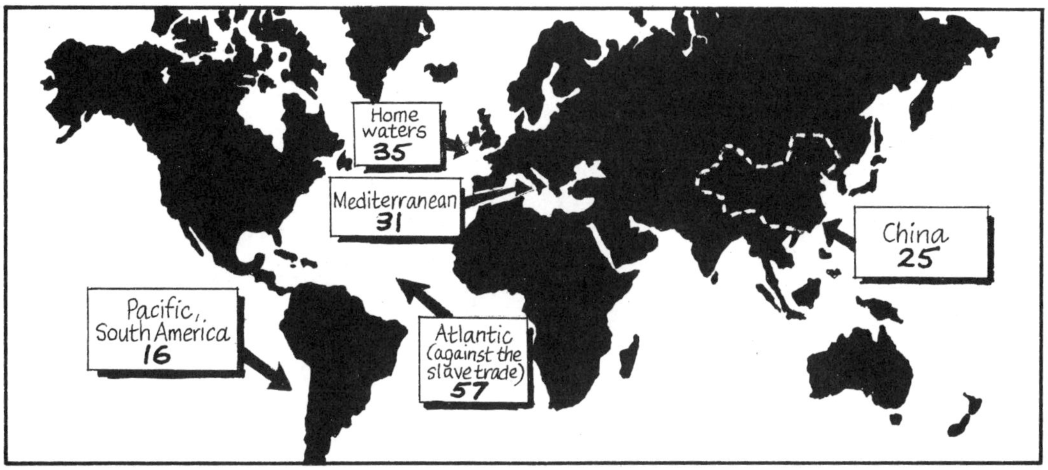

1 If each warship had two doctors, how many doctors would the Royal Navy have had on warships?

2 If each overseas warship flew three flags, how many flags would the Royal Navy have flown on its overseas warships?

3 If the warships in the Atlantic had each picked up 35 slaves, how many would they have rescued altogether?

4 If Russia, France and the USA had each had the same number of warships as the Royal Navy, how many would these three navies have had altogether?

CHECK IT YOURSELF ✓

Your answer to 1 → □□□

Your answer to 2 → □□□

Your answer to 3 → □□□□

Your answer to 4 → □□□

Add them Result → □□□□

Do you get **3202**? *If not, check your answers and try again.*

Worker Worms

Many low-paid workers worked in London. In eighteen hundred and sixty, work began on the world's first underground railway, the Metropolitan Railway. Look at this map of the line. The distances are in miles.

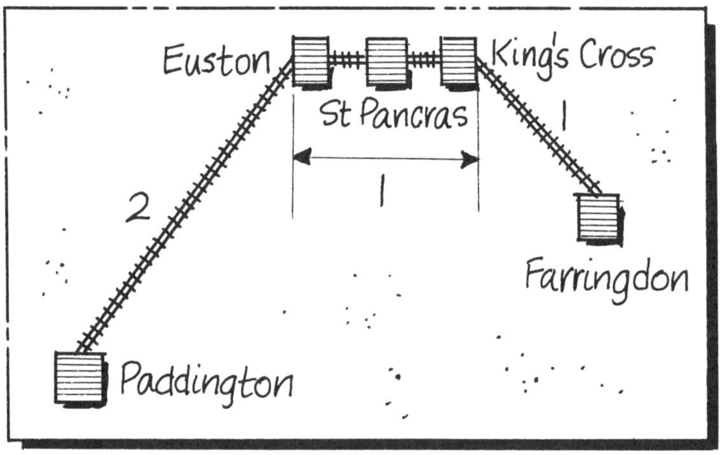

1 In what year was the Metropolitan line started? Write the number in figures.

2 How many miles long was the Metropolitan line?

3 If 12 people got on at Paddington, 23 at Euston, 11 at St Pancras, 14 at King's Cross and nobody got off, how many arrived at Farringdon?

4 If 55 people got on at Farringdon, 13 got off at King's Cross, 17 at St Pancras, 19 at Euston and nobody else got on, how many arrived at Paddington?

5 If 285 passengers travelled on one train but 39 did not pay, how many tickets were sold?

CHECK IT YOURSELF ✓

Your answer to 1 →	☐	☐	☐	☐
Your answer to 2 →				☐
Your answer to 3 →			☐	☐
Your answer to 4 →				☐
Your answer to 5 →		2	☐	☐
Add them Result →	2	1	☐	☐

Do you get **2176***?*
If not, check your answers and try again.

Worker Worms

By the mid-nineteenth century, London's population had reached three million. Many low-paid workers were needed in offices. In 1860, work started on the world's first underground railway that was not in a mine. The Metropolitan Railway linked Paddington, Euston, St Pancras and King's Cross stations, with the end of the line at Farringdon. To save important buildings owned by the rich, the line was mostly built under streets. But the homes of twelve thousand poor people were destroyed. Look at this map of the Metropolitan Railway. The distances are in miles.

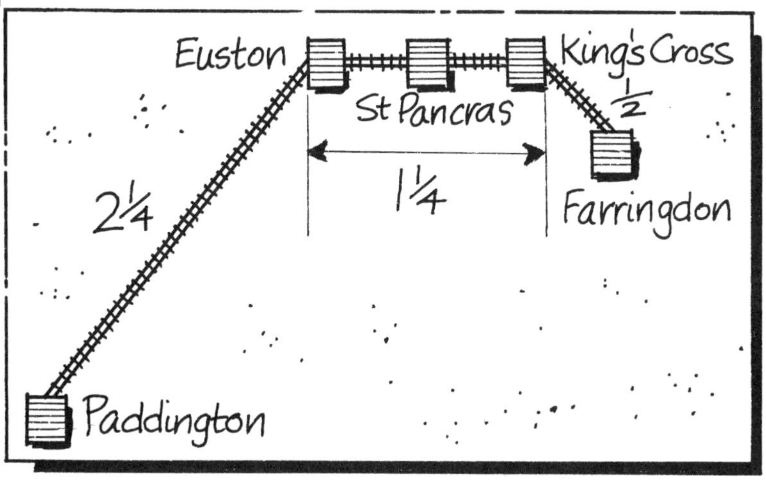

1 If you went from Farringdon to Paddington and back, how many times would you enter a station?

2 How many miles long was the one-way trip?

3 If a wagon could take 42 passengers and two-thirds of them were standing, how many were seated?

4 If a train consisted of six full wagons, how many people could it carry?

5 How many people lost their homes as a result of the new railway? Write the number in figures.

CHECK IT YOURSELF ✓

Your answer to 1 → ☐

Your answer to 2 → ☐

Your answer to 3 → ☐☐

Your answer to 4 → ☐☐☐

Your answer to 5 → ☐☐☐☐☐

Add them/Result → 1 2 ☐☐☐

Do you get **12 278**? *If not, check your answers and try again.*

Worker Worms

London boomed at the centre of the Victorian Empire. By mid-century, its population had reached three million, the biggest in the world. Many low-paid workers were needed in offices. Smart people in gowns and top hats did not want to rub shoulders with them. Therefore in 1860, work started on the world's first underground railway that was not in a mine. The Metropolitan Railway linked Paddington, Euston, St Pancras and King's Cross stations, with a terminus at Farringdon, near the busy Smithfield market. To save important buildings owned by the rich, the line was mostly built under streets. By contrast, poor people's homes were considered unimportant, so 1000 houses were destroyed, displacing 12 000 people. Look at this map of the Metropolitan Railway. The distances are in miles.

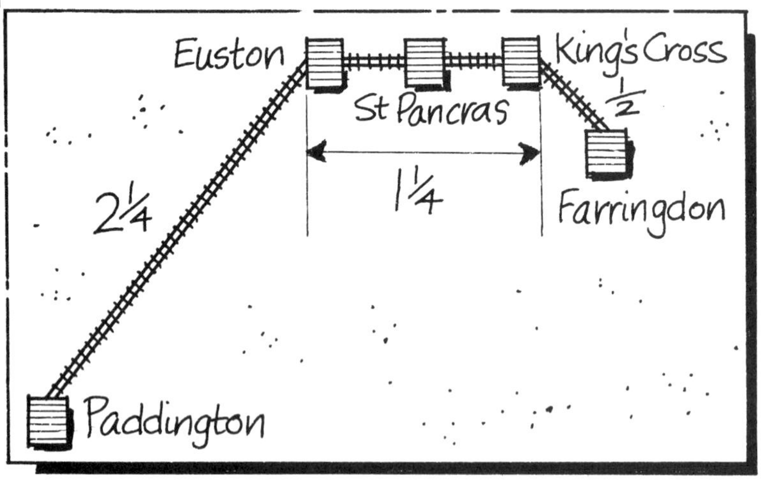

1 How many miles was it from Paddington to Farringdon, and back to Euston?

2 If the train travelled at eight miles an hour, how many hours would it take to travel the whole line one way without stopping?

3 If a wagon could take 50 passengers and 20 per cent of them were seated, how many were standing?

4 If a full train carried 252 passengers, how many passengers did eight trains carry?

5 If 180 people travelled in a train but ten per cent of them did not pay, how many tickets were sold?

VICTORIAN FACT FILE
The first carriages on the underground train were open wagons. The passengers travelled in them through the dark. At least the locomotives had special pipes taking steam and smoke away into a tank.

CHECK IT YOURSELF ✓

Your answer to 1 ⟶ ☐ ☐

Your answer to 2 ⟶ ☐

Your answer to 3 ⟶ ☐ ☐

Your answer to 4 ⟶ ☐ ☐ ☐ ☐

Your answer to 5 ⟶ ☐ ☐ ☐

Add them Result ⟶ ☐ ☐ ☐ ☐ ☐

Do you get **$2224\frac{1}{4}$**? *If not, check your answers and try again.*

Corner Clones

Workers spent their wages in shops. A new type of shop was the chain store, with hundreds of identical shops up and down the country. In 1880, there were one thousand five hundred chain stores in Britain.

1 How many chain stores were there in 1880? Write the number in figures.

2 A local family business asks £12 for a pair of shoes. A new chain store sells similar ones for £10. How many pounds cheaper is the chain-store pair?

3 A corner shop has 35 chocolates in its chocolate-box. The chain store has 42 for the same price. How many more are in the chain-store box?

4 A local shop asks £118 to furnish a house. A chain store offers to do the same job for £89. How many pounds more expensive is the local shop?

5 The local chemist sells 82 tablets for two shillings. The chain chemist does a jar of 105 for the same price. How many more do you get?

CHECK IT YOURSELF ✓

Your answer to 1 → ☐ ☐ ☐ ☐

Your answer to 2 → ☐

Your answer to 3 → ☐

Your answer to 4 → ☐ ☐

Your answer to 5 → ☐ ☐

Add them Result → **1** **5** ☐ ☐

Do you get **1561***?*
If not, check your answers and try again.

Corner Clones

Workers had to buy everything they needed, so they spent their wages in shops. A new type of shop was the chain store, with hundreds of identical shops up and down the country. By buying and selling in big amounts, the owners could drive down prices and close local family businesses. In 1880, there were 1500 chain stores in Britain. By 1897, there were 11 000.

1 If there were 125 chain stores in Manchester in 1880 and 650 by 1897, by how many had the number increased?

2 A high-street chain store sells four candles for eight pence. The local family business sells five similar ones for 15 pence. How many pence cheaper is one chain-store candle?

3 A local store offers a whistling kettle for six shillings. The chain store is offering a half-price deal. How much is their kettle?

4 A local shop asks £395 to furnish a house. A chain store offers to do the same job for £299. How many pounds more expensive is the local shop?

5 The local chemist sells 182 tablets for two shillings. The chain chemist does a jar of 205 for the same price. How many more do you get?

CHECK IT YOURSELF ✓

Your answer to 1 → ☐☐☐

Your answer to 2 → ☐

Your answer to 3 → ☐

Your answer to 4 → ☐☐

Your answer to 5 → ☐☐

Add them Result → ☐☐☐

Do you get ***648****?*
If not, check your answers and try again.

Corner Clones

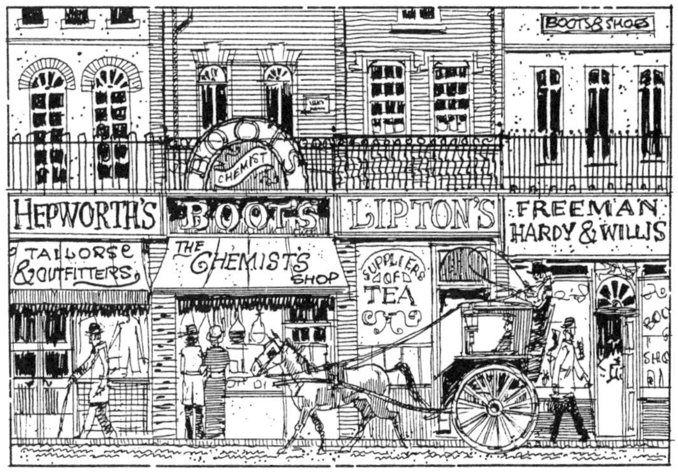

Workers in the 'workshop of the world' no longer had their own land or time to make their own clothes. They had to buy everything they needed, so they spent their wages in shops. Financiers quickly invented the chain store and built hundreds of identical outlets up and down the country. By buying and selling in big amounts, the owners could drive down prices and close local family businesses. In 1880, there were 1500 chain stores in Britain. By 1897, there were 11 000.

1 If there were 1425 chain stores in 1880 and 9450 five years later, by how many had the number increased?

2 A local family business offers to fit new windows for £100. The high-street chain store offers a one-quarter discount. How many pounds cheaper is the chain-store price?

VICTORIAN FACT FILE
Among the early chain stores were: Lipton's, the grocer's; Freeman, Hardy & Willis, the shoe shop; Boot's, the chemist's; and Hepworth's, the tailor's. Public education had taught most people to read. The chain stores could attract them with advertisements. Soon, advertising was big business.

3 A local store offers a whistling kettle for six shillings. The chain store is offering a 50 per cent discount. How much is their kettle?

4 A local shop asks £400 to furnish a house. A chain store offers to do the same job for 25 per cent less. How many pounds cheaper is the chain store?

5 The local chemist sells 1250 pills for two shillings. The chain chemist does a jar of 1345 for the same price. How many more do you get?

CHECK IT YOURSELF ✓

Your answer to 1 → □□□□

Your answer to 2 → □□

Your answer to 3 → □

Your answer to 4 → □□□

Your answer to 5 → □□

Add them Result → □□□□

Do you get ***8248****?*
If not, check your answers and try again.

Phoney Talk

The first telephone exchange opened in London in eighteen hundred and seventy-nine. It was just three years since Alexander Graham Bell had shown his telephone in the USA.

STATELLITE
Here are some London exchange names and the number of calls that might have been made through them every minute.

Whitehall	86	Abbey	41
Welbeck	32	Avenue	53

1 In what year was London's first telephone exchange built? Write the number in figures.

2 In what year had Bell demonstrated his telephone?

3 How many calls were handled per minute on the four exchanges listed?

4 If the Welbeck exchange broke down, how many calls per minute were handled on the remaining three exchanges?

5 How many calls were handled on the Abbey exchange in two minutes?

CHECK IT YOURSELF ✓

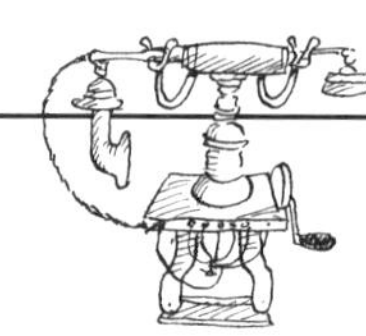

Your answer to 1 →	☐	☐	☐	☐
Your answer to 2 →	☐	☐	☐	☐
Your answer to 3 →		**2**	☐	☐
Your answer to 4 →		**1**	☐	☐
Your answer to 5 →			☐	☐
Add them Result →	**4**	**2**	☐	☐

Do you get **4229**? *If not, check your answers and try again.*

Phoney Talk

The first telephone exchange opened in London in 1879. It was just three years since Alexander Graham Bell had shown his telephone in the USA.

STATELLITE
Here are some London exchange names and the number of calls that might have been made through them every minute.

Whitehall	86
Welbeck	32
Abbey	41
Avenue	53

1 How many calls were made through the Whitehall exchange in eight minutes?

2 How many calls were made through the Welbeck exchange in seven minutes?

3 How many calls were handled per half-minute on the Whitehall exchange?

4 How many calls were handled every fifteen seconds on the Welbeck exchange?

5 How many calls were handled on the Abbey exchange in five minutes?

VICTORIAN FACT FILE
One example of a telephone number linked to an exchange name is that of London's Metropolitan Police which for many years was Whitehall 1212.

CHECK IT YOURSELF ✓

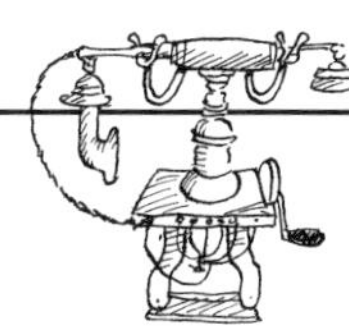

Your answer to 1 → ☐☐☐

Your answer to 2 → ☐☐☐

Your answer to 3 → ☐☐

Your answer to 4 → ☐

Your answer to 5 → ☐☐☐

Add them/Result → ☐☐☐☐

Do you get **1168**? *If not, check your answers and try again.*

Phoney Talk

The first telephone exchange opened in London in 1879. It was just three years since Alexander Graham Bell had demonstrated his telephone in the USA. (His fellow American, Elisha Gray, also invented it, but Bell won the patent.) Telephone numbers originally went by the name of their telephone exchange. A connection was made by the operator plugging or 'patching' a wire into the right exchange socket.

STATELLITE

Here are some London exchange names and the number of calls that might have been made through them every minute.

Whitehall	186
Welbeck	132
Abbey	141
Avenue	153

1 How many calls were made through the Whitehall exchange in eight minutes?

2 How many calls were made through the Welbeck exchange in seven minutes?

3 How many calls were handled per half-minute on the Whitehall exchange?

4 How many calls were handled every fifteen seconds on the Welbeck exchange?

5 How many calls were handled on the Abbey exchange in five minutes?

VICTORIAN FACT FILE

One example of a telephone number linked to an exchange name is that of London's Metropolitan Police which for many years was Whitehall 1212.

CHECK IT YOURSELF ✓

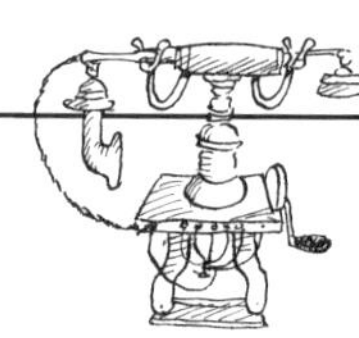

Your answer to 1 → ☐☐☐☐

Your answer to 2 → ☐☐☐

Your answer to 3 → ☐☐

Your answer to 4 → ☐☐

Your answer to 5 → ☐☐☐

Add them Result → ☐☐☐☐

Do you get **3243**? *If not, check your answers and try again.*

The Sun Never Sets

At the end of Queen Victoria's reign in 1901, a quarter of the world's people lived under British rule. There was a saying at the time: 'The sun never sets on the British Empire.' The map shows the number of countries under British rule in each area.

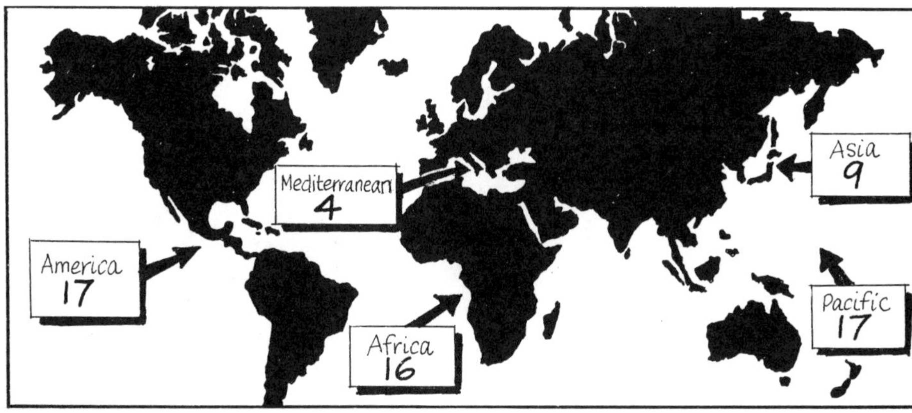

1 How many countries in Africa and the Pacific were part of the British Empire?

2 How many countries in America, Asia and the Mediterranean were part of the British Empire?

3 How many more countries were part of the Empire in America than in the Mediterranean?

4 How many more countries were part of the Empire in the Pacific than in Asia?

5 How many countries altogether were part of the Empire (not counting the UK and Ireland)?

CHECK IT YOURSELF ✓

Your answer to 1 → ☐☐

Your answer to 2 → ☐☐

Your answer to 3 → ☐☐

Your answer to 4 → ☐

Your answer to 5 → ☐☐

Add them Result → ☐☐☐

Do you get **147**? *If not, check your answers and try again.*

The Sun Never Sets

At the end of Queen Victoria's reign in 1901, a quarter of the world's population lived under British rule. The Union Jack flag flew over nearly half of Africa, as well as all the Indian subcontinent. There was a saying at the time: 'The sun never sets on the British Empire.' The map shows the number of countries under British rule in each area.

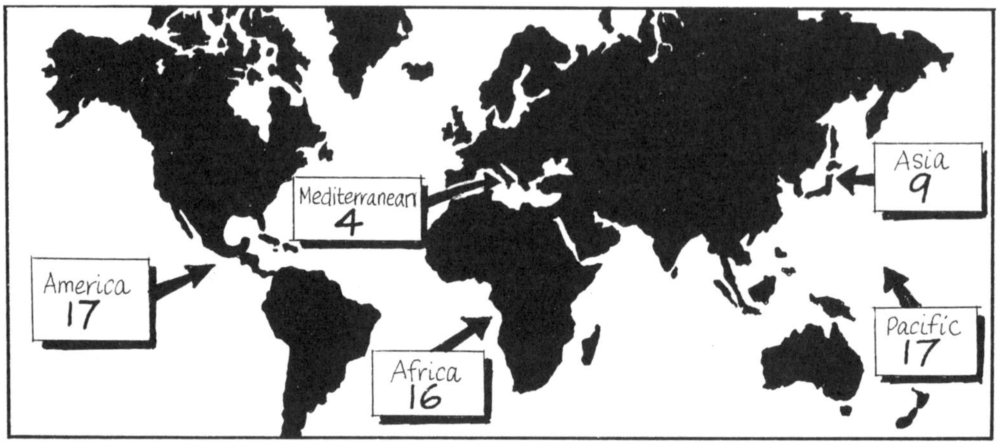

1 What fraction of the world's population did not live under British rule?

2 If the Foreign Office had two buildings in each country, how many buildings would it have had to maintain?

3 If the Prime Minister visited each of the African countries three times, how many visits would he have made?

4 If eight people in each of the Pacific countries reached the age of 100, how many birthday telegrams would Queen Victoria have had to send?

5 Imagine all the American countries had sent five sprinters to the Empire Games. How many sprinters would have come?

CHECK IT YOURSELF ✓

Your answer to 2 → ☐ ☐ ☐

Your answer to 3 → ☐ ☐

Your answer to 4 → ☐ ☐ ☐

Your answer to 5 → ☐ ☐

Add them Result → ☐ ☐ ☐

Do you get **395**?
If not, check your answers and try again.

The Sun Never Sets

At the end of Queen Victoria's reign in 1901, a quarter of the world's population lived under British rule. The Empire covered one-fifth of the planet's land. Colonies had been unpopular early in the Queen's reign because they cost money. Later, the British believed they had a mission to civilise the world. The Union Jack flag flew over nearly half of the African continent, as well as all the Indian subcontinent. There was a saying at the time: 'The sun never sets on the British Empire.' The map shows the number of countries under British rule in each area.

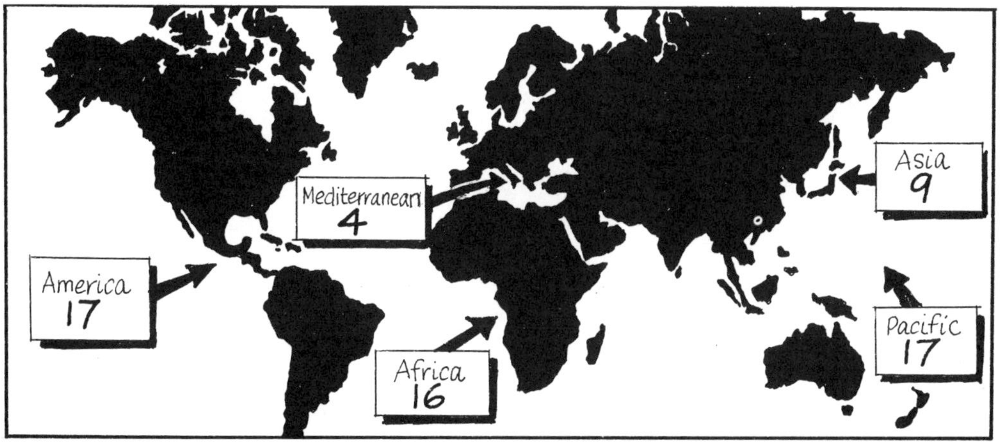

1 If each African country had sent a cricket team (of 11) to the Empire Games, how many players would have come?

2 If the Foreign Office had had 12 carriages in each country, how many carriages would it have owned?

3 If the Prime Minister had sent 14 letters to each of the Pacific countries, how many would his secretaries have had to write?

4 If 23 people in each of the American countries had reached the age of 100, how many telegrams would Queen Victoria have had to send?

5 Suppose all the Empire countries had sent four athletes to the Empire games. One in three of them caught flu and had to stay in bed. How many would have competed?

CHECK IT YOURSELF ✓

Your answer to 1 →

Your answer to 2 →

Your answer to 3 →

Your answer to 4 →

Your answer to 5 →

Add them Result →

Do you get ***1729****?*
If not, check your answers and try again.

Answers

Steam Trains

Level 1
1 1838
2 12 + 23 = 35
3 112 + 90 = 202
4 112 + 122 = 224
5 London to Birmingham; 112 – 102 = 10

Level 2
1 112 + 90 + 12 = 214
2 12 + 23 = 35 x 4 = 140
3 112 + 90 = 202 + 202 = 404
4 112 + 112 = 224 + 224 = 448
5 London to Birmingham; 112 + 112 = 224; 102 + 102 = 204; 224 – 204 = 20

Level 3
1 214 + 214 = 428
2 12 + 23 = 35 x 2 = 70 x 7 = 490
3 112 + 90 = 202 + 202 = 404
4 112 + 112 = 224 x 3 = 672
5 90 + 12 = 102 x 2 = 204

Any New Iron?

Level 1
1 280
2 $\frac{1}{2}$
3 31 + 31 + 31 = 93
4 2 x $\frac{1}{2}$ = 1

Level 2
1 280 + 280 = 560
2 30 ÷ 3 = 10
3 30 x 8 = 240
4 2 x 7 = 14

Level 3
1 280 x 5 = 1400
2 30 x $\frac{3}{4}$ = 22$\frac{1}{2}$
3 30 x 18 = 540
4 2700 + 2700 + 2700 = 8100

Clip-clop Buses

Level 1
1 6000
2 24 + 24 = 48
3 8 x 3 = 24
4 24 – 5 = 19
5 24 + 24 = 48 – (12 + 9 = 21) = 48 – 21 = 27

Level 2
1 1858
2 24 ÷ 2 = 12
3 28 x 3 = 84
4 24 – (24 x $\frac{1}{4}$ = 6) = 24 – 6 = 18
5 24 x 3 = 72 – (12 x 3 = 36) = 72 – 36 = 36

Level 3
1 600 x 3 = 1800
2 600 – (600 ÷ 3 = 200) = 600 – 200 = 400
3 28 x 24 = 672
4 6000 + 6000 = 12 000
5 24 x 11 = 264 – (12 x 11 = 132) = 264 – 132 = 132

Answers

Mine Martyrs

Level 1

1. 10 – 4 = 6
2. $1 - \frac{3}{4} = \frac{1}{4}$
3. 23 – 7 = 16
4. 180 – 75 = 105
5. 245 – 47 = 198

Level 2

1. 1 – 0.3 = 0.7
2. 1 – 0.75 = 0.25
3. 342 + 247 = 589
4. 35 x 8 = 280
5. 18 – (18 ÷ 3 = 6) = 18 – 6 = 12

Level 3

1. 300 ÷ 2 = 150
2. 100 – 75 = 25
3. 2342 + 4577 = 6919
4. 35 x 18 = 630
5. 129 – (129 ÷ 3 = 43) = 129 – 43 = 86

Super-ship

Level 1

1. 252
2. (18)45 – 7 = (18)38 = 1838
3. (18)45 + 7 = (18)52 = 1852
4. (18)66 – (18)52 = 14
5. 15

Level 2

1. 1843
2. 252 + 92 = 344
3. 24 – 21 = 3
4. (18)66 – (18)45 = 21
5. 344 + 344 = 688

Level 3

1. 1110 + 1200 = 2310
2. 252 + 92 = 344 x 8 = 2752
3. 112(000) ÷ 2 = 56(000) = 56 000
4. 14 x 24 = 336 + 21 = 357
5. 12 ÷ 3 = 4 x 7 = 28

Pedalling Along

Level 1

1. 12 x 2 = 24
2. 4(00) ÷ 2 = 2(00) = 200
3. 100 x 3 = 300
4. 9 x 2 = 18

Level 2

1. 24 x 2 = 48
2. 400 + 400 + 400 = 1200
3. 100 ÷ 2 = 50
4. 39 x 2 = 78

Level 3

1. 1865 – 1818 = 47
2. 400 x 9 = 3600
3. 392 x 2 = 784
4. 1888 – 1846 = 42
5. $100 \times \frac{30}{100} = 30$

Answers

Crystal Palace

Level 1
1. 244
2. 14 ÷ 2 = 7
3. 1851 + 5 = 1856
4. 3 x 2 = 6

Level 2
1. 244 ÷ 2 = 122
2. 14 x 4 = 56
3. 14 000
4. 3 x 36 = 108

Level 3
1. 5 x 1.5 = 7.5
2. 24.4 = 24
3. 14 000 + 14 000 + 14 000 + 14 000 = 56 000
4. 36 ÷ 12 = 3 + 1851 = 1854

A Bright Idea

Level 1
1. 30 + 25 + 60 = 115
2. 115 – 25 = 90
3. 75 + 75 + 75 + 75 = 300
4. 30 + 30 + 30 + 30 = 120
5. 65 + 65 = 130

Level 2
1. 90 + 125 + 150 = 365
2. 365 – 125 = 240
3. 75 x 8 = 600
4. 365 + 365 = 730
5. 150 + 150 = 300

Level 3
1. 90 + 125 + 150 = 365 x 4 = 1460
2. 1460 – 125 = 1335
3. 75 x 4 = 300 x 8 = 2400
4. 60 x 4 = 240 x 8 = 1920
5. 30 x 2 = 60 + (55 x 60 = 3300) = 60 + 3300 = 3360

Naval Empire

Level 1
1. 31 + 16 + 57 + 25 = 129
2. 129 + 35 = 164
3. 164 – 57 = 107
4. 25 + 16 = 41

Level 2
1. 25 x 2 = 50
2. 57 x 3 = 171
3. 35 + 31 + 16 + 57 + 25 = 164
4. 25 + 16 = 41 x 3 = 123

Level 3
1. 35 + 31 + 16 + 57 + 25 = 164 x 2 = 328
2. 16 + 57 + 25 + 31 = 129 x 3 = 387
3. 57 x 35 = 1995
4. 164 x 3 = 492

Answers

Worker Worms

Level 1

1 1860
2 2 + 1 + 1 = 4
3 12 + 23 + 11 + 14 = 60
4 55 – 13 = 42 – 17 = 25 – 19 = 6
5 285 – 39 = 246

Level 2

1 8
2 $2\frac{1}{4} + 1\frac{1}{4} + \frac{1}{2} = 4$
3 $42 \times \frac{1}{3} = 42 \div 3 = 14$
4 6 x 42 = 252
5 12 000

Level 3

1 $2\frac{1}{4} + 1\frac{1}{4} + \frac{1}{2} + \frac{1}{2} + 1\frac{1}{4} = 5\frac{3}{4}$
2 $2\frac{1}{4} + 1\frac{1}{4} + \frac{1}{2} = 4 \div 8 = \frac{4}{8} = \frac{1}{2}$
3 $50 - (50 \times \frac{20}{100} = \frac{1000}{100} = 10)$
$= 50 - 10 = 40$
4 8 x 252 = 2016
5 $180 - (180 \times \frac{10}{100} = 18)$
$= 180 - 18 = 162$

Corner Clones

Level 1

1 1500
2 12 – 10 = 2
3 42 – 35 = 7
4 118 – 89 = 29
5 105 – 82 = 23

Level 2

1 650 – 125 = 525
2 8 ÷ 4 = 2; 15 ÷ 5 = 3; 3 – 2 = 1
3 6 ÷ 2 = 3
4 395 – 299 = 96
5 205 – 182 = 23

Level 3

1 9450 – 1425 = 8025
2 $100 - (100 \times \frac{75}{100} = 75) = 100 - 75 = 25$
3 $6 \times \frac{50}{100} = 3$
4 $400 \times \frac{25}{100} = 100$
5 1345 – 1250 = 95

Phoney Talk

Level 1

1 1879
2 (18)79 – 3 = (18)76 = 1876
3 86 + 32 + 41 + 53 = 212
4 212 – 32 = 180
5 41 + 41 = 82

Level 2

1 8 x 86 = 688
2 7 x 32 = 224
3 86 ÷ 2 = 43
4 32 ÷ 4 = 8
5 41 x 5 = 205

Level 3

1 8 x 186 = 1488
2 7 x 132 = 924
3 186 ÷ 2 = 93
4 132 ÷ 4 = 33
5 141 x 5 = 705

Answers

The Sun Never Sets

Level 1

1 16 + 17 = 33
2 17 + 9 + 4 = 30
3 17 – 4 = 13
4 17 – 9 = 8
5 4 + 9 + 16 + 17 + 17 = 63

Level 2

1 $1 - \frac{1}{4} = \frac{3}{4}$
2 4 + 9 + 16 + 17 + 17 = 63 x 2 = 126
3 16 x 3 = 48
4 17 x 8 = 136
5 17 x 5 = 85

Level 3

1 16 x 11 = 176
2 4 + 9 + 16 + 17 + 17 = 63 x 12 = 756
3 17 x 14 = 238
4 17 x 23 = 391
5 4 + 9 + 16 + 17 + 17 = 63 x 4
= 252 – (252 ÷ 3 = 84)
= 252 – 84 = 168

